Polar Bears

Gee Johnson

Look at the polar bear.

Look at the eyes.

ear

Look at the ears.

Look at the nose.

Look at the mouth.

Look at the tongue.

fur

Look at the fur.

paw

Look at the paw.

Look at the babies.

snow

Look at the snow.

Water

Look at the water.

seal

Look at the seal.

fish

Look at the fish.

wolf

Look at the wolf.

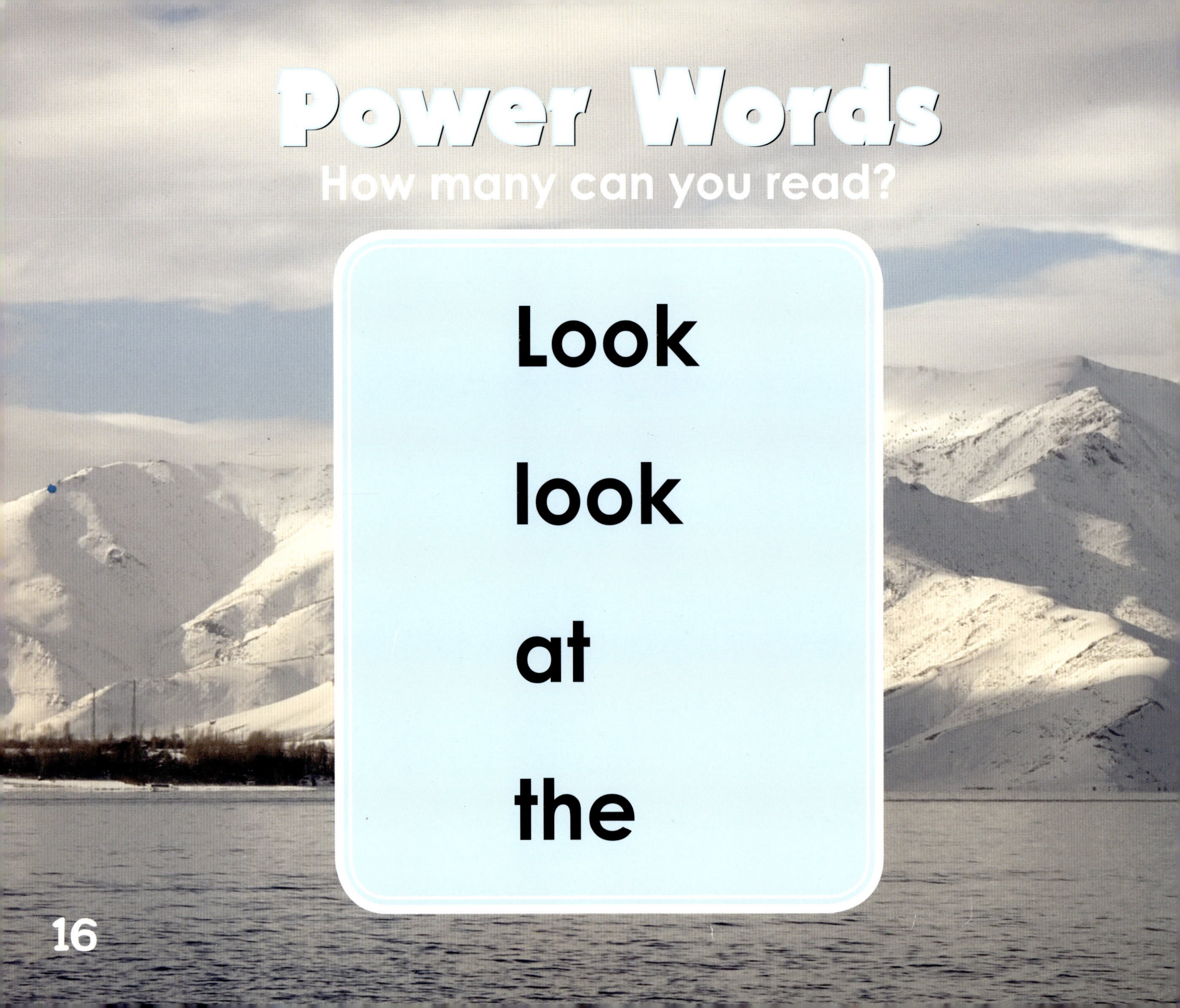

Power Words

How many can you read?

Look

look

at

the